FOOD CRAFTS

By Chris Deshpande
Photographs by Zul Mukhida

Contents

Gareth Stevens Publishing
MILWAUKEE

About this book

Did you know that some of the dyes we use to color fabric come from vegetables and spices? This book is about food and cooking from around the world. It shows you how to make crafts based on food and gives you plenty of ideas to help you design your own.

In this book, you can find out about customs, crafts, and traditions based on food. At the back of the book, there is information on how to find out more about these crafts and traditions, with details about places to visit and books to read.

Some of the craft activities in this book are more complicated than others and will take longer to finish. It might be fun to ask some friends to help with these activities, such as making salt dough beads on page 6.

Before you start working on any of the craft projects, read through the instructions carefully. Each step-by-step instruction has a number. Look for the same number in the picture to see how to make each stage of your model.

Before you begin

Collect everything listed in the "You will need" box.

Ask an adult's permission if you are going to use a sharp tool, dye cloth, or use an oven.

Prepare a clear work surface.

If the activity is going to be messy, cover the surface with old newspaper or a waterproof sheet.

3

Pretzels

Pretzels are a kind of hard bread baked in knot shapes with a salty coating. They come from Germany where they were traditionally eaten at carnival time. Now they are eaten all year round as snacks. Many people believe pretzels were first made by a baker who was imprisoned for selling bad bread. He was told that he could go free if he baked something that let the sun shine through it three times. He baked pretzels.

Try making some pretzels

You will need:
- a small saucepan
- two small bowls
- a mixing bowl
- a measuring cup
- a sieve
- a fork
- a clean cloth
- a cookie sheet
- a pastry brush
- a spoon
- an oven
- 1/4 teaspoon (1.2 ml) dried yeast
- 1/4 teaspoon (1.2 ml) cinnamon
- 1/8 cup (25 g) sugar
- 1/4 cup (50 g) butter
- 1/2 cup (125 ml) milk
- 1 egg
- 1-1/8 cup (275 g) flour
- a pinch of sea salt

1 **Ask an adult to help you make the pretzels.** Wash your hands. Heat the milk in the saucepan until it is just lukewarm. Pour the milk into a small bowl and stir in the dried yeast and sugar. Leave the mixture in a warm place for about 10 minutes, until it's frothy. Wash the saucepan.

2 Sift the flour, cinnamon, and salt into the mixing bowl. Make a well in the middle and pour in the yeast mixture.

3 Break the egg into a bowl and beat it with a fork. Save some of the egg for later. Gently heat the butter in a saucepan until it is runny. Pour the butter and egg into the flour mixture.

4 Mix it together with your hands. Sprinkle some flour onto a clean kitchen surface and fold and press, or knead, the dough for about 5 minutes. Cover the dough with the cloth and let it rise for about 20 minutes.

5 Divide the dough into small balls and roll them into long sausage shapes. Can you make shapes that will let the sun shine through three times? Put the pretzels on the cookie sheet. Let them rise in a warm place for 20 minutes. Set the oven to 425°F (220°C).

Brush the pretzels with beaten egg and sprinkle with sea salt. Bake them in the oven for 10 minutes, until they are brown.

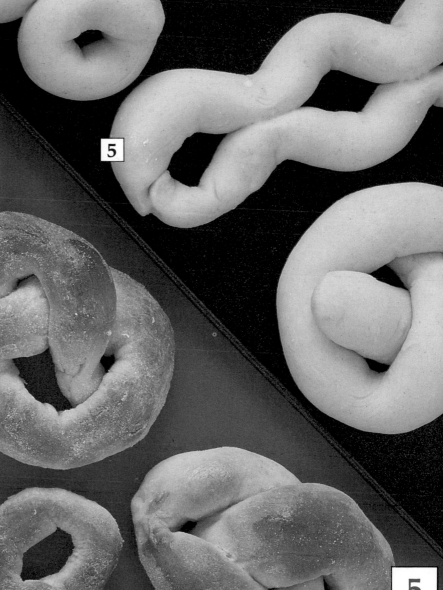

5

Salt dough beads

Dough is something we usually think of as food. Bread, pastry, and cookies are made from sweet dough, but salt dough is not meant to be eaten. It can be used to make models, beads, and jewelry.

Try making some salt dough jewelry. Before you begin, look at the shapes and colors of different kinds of beads and pendants to get some ideas for your own designs.

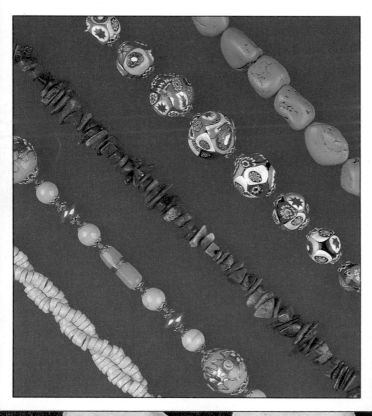

You will need:
- 1 cup (200 grams) flour
- 2 tablespoons (30 ml) salt
- water
- a mixing bowl
- a darning needle
- a cookie sheet
- paintbrushes
- paints
- cord, thick thread, or shirring elastic
- an oven set at 300°F (150°C)

1 Put the flour and salt in a bowl. Add a little bit of water, stir the mixture, and add some more water until you have a stiff dough. Fold and press, or knead, the dough for about five minutes.

2 Break off a small piece of dough and roll or press it into the size and shape bead you want. Push a thick darning needle through the center of the bead. Make many more beads in this way. Experiment making different sized and shaped beads.

3 Place the beads on the tray and **ask an adult to put it in the oven** for about an hour.

4 When the beads are cool, paint them. Thread the needle with cord and tie a knot at the end. Thread your beads onto the cord. Tie the ends of the cord together.

You can make an interesting shape from salt dough for a pendant. Or try threading small beads onto shirring elastic to make a hair tie or bracelet.

4

7

Milk painting

In the seventeenth century, many Europeans traveled to North America to settle. Often, they traveled thousands of miles before reaching their final destination, and they carried very little with them. When the settlers arrived, they made furniture and household utensils out of wood from trees they cut down themselves. Sometimes they decorated the wood with a special kind of paint made from milk, and fruit and vegetable dyes. This milk paint dried to a very hard finish. Some of this milk-painted furniture has lasted for over three hundred years.

Try decorating a wooden fruit crate with milk paint

You will need:
- a tablespoon
- a bowl
- warm water
- paintbrushes
- varnish
- sandpaper
- nonfat milk powder
- a hammer
- an old wooden fruit crate
- food coloring, including turmeric

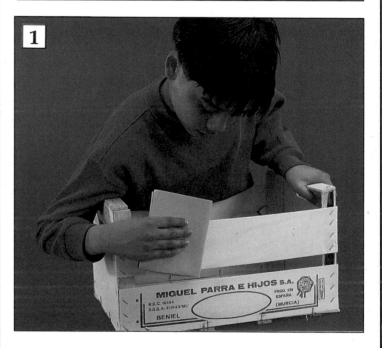

1 Smooth the rough surfaces of the crate with sandpaper. Hammer in any nails that stick out.

2 Put about 2 tablespoons (30 ml) of milk powder into the bowl. Add small amounts of water until you make a thick, smooth paste. Add a few drops of food coloring or 1/2 teaspoon (2.5 ml) of turmeric to the mixture. You can make different shades of color by using different amounts of food coloring.

3 Try painting big shapes in colored milk paint on the box. Let the paint dry for about ten hours. Then give the box a coat of varnish to add gloss and take away the milky smell. You can use the box as a toy box or bookshelf.

Natural dyes

Some colors have special meanings. In ancient Rome, for example, only the caesars could wear purple, a color that came from an expensive dye made from shellfish. And traditionally, the robes of Buddhist monks were dyed yellow with saffron, which comes from crocuses.

For thousands of years, people have experimented with dyes to color their clothes. Dyes can be made from fruits and vegetables, berries, herbs, flowers, twigs, and bark.

Ask an adult to help you dye an old pair of cotton socks with beets, red cabbage, or turmeric. The dye will work best on white cotton material. And remember always to wash your dyed clothes separately in case the dye runs.

You will need:
- a knife
- a chopping board
- water
- salt
- rubber gloves
- a sieve
- a saucepan that isn't enamel
- a pair of old, white cotton socks

One of the following:
- 2 teaspoons (10 ml) of turmeric
- half a large, red cabbage or one large, uncooked beet

1 Put a washed beet in the saucepan with 1 quart (1 liter) of water. Bring the water to a boil and simmer for about 30 minutes. Take the beet out of the saucepan. You can peel the beet and eat it in a salad.

Carefully sieve the beet water into a bowl. Stir 4 tablespoons (60 ml) of salt into the water. Put the socks and water back into the saucepan. Simmer for about 20 minutes. Remove from heat.

When the saucepan is cool, put it in the sink. Wear rubber gloves and rinse the socks in cold water. Hang them up to dry.

2 Try dyeing a pair of socks with red cabbage. Slice up the cabbage, then follow the instructions for dyeing with beets, but use cabbage water instead.

3 Put 2 teaspoons (10 ml) of turmeric into a saucepan with 1 quart (1 l) of cold water. Bring the water to a boil. Stir about 4 tablespoons (60 ml) of salt into the water. Add the socks and put the saucepan back on the stove. Simmer for about 20 minutes. Remove from heat. When the saucepan is cool, put it in the sink. Wear rubber gloves and rinse the socks in cold water. Hang them up to dry.

Flour-and-water paste batik

Batik is a way of decorating fabric. A design is painted on the fabric with hot wax, and then the fabric is dyed. The fabric does not take the dye where it is covered by the wax design. When the wax is removed, the design shows up clearly.

The art of batik started in China and then became popular in India and the Far East. This picture shows a man removing a hot wax batik design from fabric with an iron.

Hot wax batik can be dangerous, but you can achieve nearly the same effect with flour-and-water paste. Try decorating a handkerchief with a batik design. It's best to use a white cotton handkerchief.

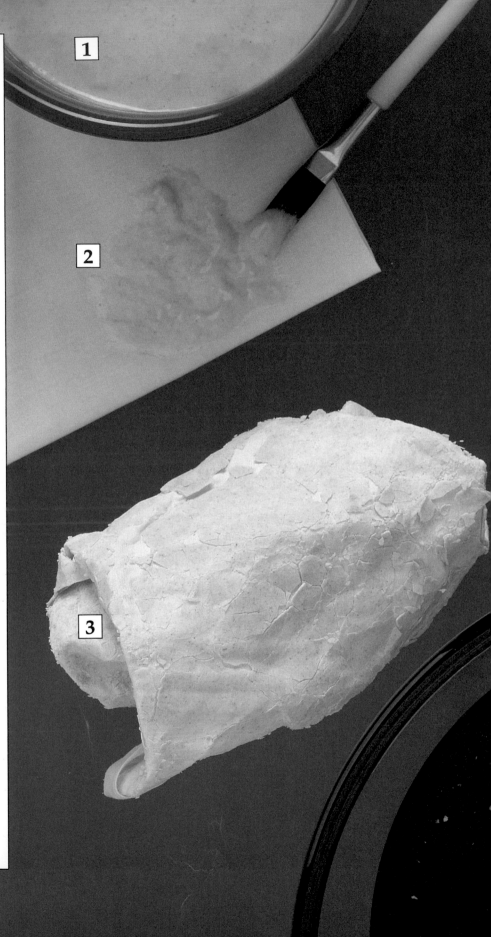

You will need:
- a mixing bowl
- flour and water
- a thick paintbrush
- a bucket
- rubber gloves
- cold water dye
- a knife
- a tablespoon
- a white cotton handkerchief

1 Mix 4 tablespoons (60 ml) of flour with 3 tablespoons (45 ml) of water to make a smooth paste.

2 Use a paintbrush to paint a thick layer of paste all over the handkerchief on both sides. Let the paste dry overnight.

3 When the handkerchief is dry, scrunch it up so that the paste cracks and looks like dry earth.

4 **Ask an adult to help you make the cold water dye in a bowl.** Follow the instructions on the packet carefully and wear rubber gloves. Soak the handkerchief in the dye for about one hour. Then take it out and rinse it thoroughly in cold water. Hang it up to dry.

5 When the handkerchief is dry, use a knife to scrape away any paste that is left. Rinse the handkerchief again, then wash it in soapy water and let it dry. Always wash your dyed handkerchief separately in case the dye runs.

Try making some different batik patterns. For example, you might paint paste circles on a handkerchief and then dye it.

5

4

Potato prints

In the 1920s, potato printing was made popular by a teacher in France. She called the craft PDT, which represents the first letters of the French word for potato, pomme de terre.

You can make complicated-looking patterns from simple potato prints. Many patterns are based on squares, circles, or triangles. Try making a printed pattern with a potato.

You will need:
- paper and pencil
- scissors
- a large potato
- four sewing pins
- a small, sharp knife
- poster paints
- a paintbrush
- paper for printing

1 Cut out a simple shape in paper that will fit on half a cut potato. Cut a pattern into your paper shape. Think about how you can repeat this shape to make a pattern.

2 **Ask an adult to help you cut the potato in half with a knife.**

3 Pin the shape to the cut surface of one half of the potato. **Ask an adult to cut away the potato around the shape.** Take the paper shape and pins off the potato.

4 Brush paint onto the raised part of the potato and press it on the paper. Here are a few suggestions for ways to make patterns. Try out your own ideas as well.

5 Repeat a print in straight rows.

6 Print in rotation, which means moving the potato print around each time like a wheel.

7 Try using two stamps to make a printed pattern.

8 Try printing a picture. To make a flower, use one stamp for the leaves, one for the stem, and another for the petals.

Try making your own gift-wrapping paper or greeting cards. If you make a small design, you can print a border for writing paper.

15

Seed necklaces

For centuries, all over the world, beads of all types have been used to make jewelry and decorate clothes and household items. In Victorian England, beads were used to decorate teapot stands and fire screens. Native Americans sewed beads onto their clothes and moccasins.

Beads are made from precious gems, shells, wood, clay, glass, nuts, berries, stones, and seeds.

Try making a melon-seed necklace

You will need:
- soapy water
- absorbent paper
- cotton sewing thread
- a darning needle
- melon seeds from about four honeydew melons
- scissors

1 Wash the melon seeds in soapy water. Rinse them and let them dry on absorbent paper for about two days.

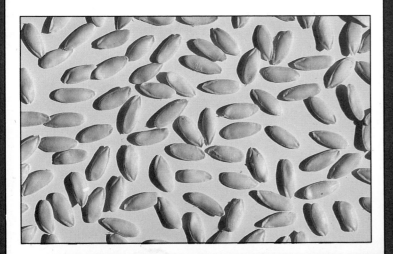

2 Drape some cotton thread around your neck and decide how long you want your necklace to be. Measure half as much again. Cut three pieces of thread to this length. Tie them together at one end. Thread all three lengths of thread through the darning needle.

3 Push the needle through about fifteen melon seeds and slide them down to the knot.

4 Pull out two of the strands of cotton from the eye of the needle. Thread about fifteen seeds onto the first strand of thread that is still in the needle.

5 Pull out the first strand from the needle and thread the needle with the second strand. Push about fifteen seeds onto this strand.

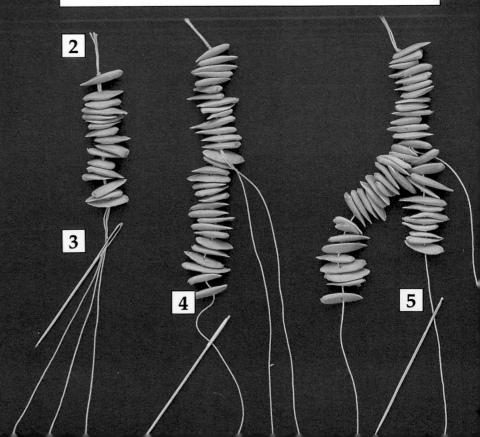

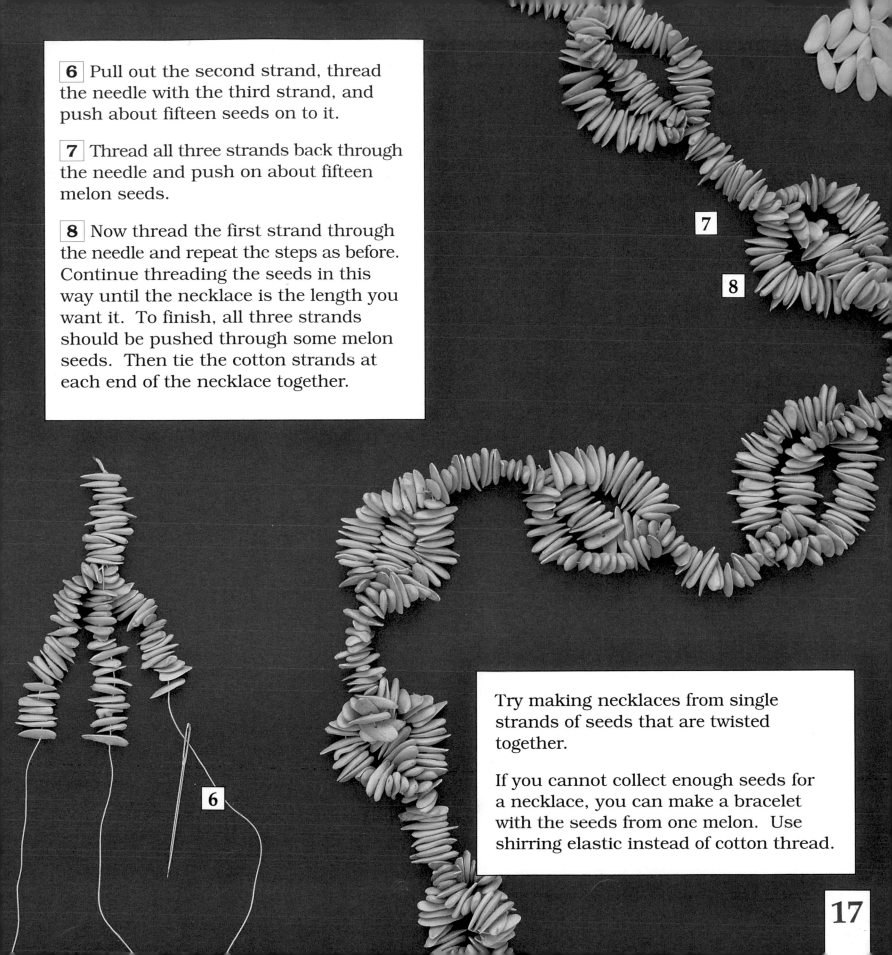

6 Pull out the second strand, thread the needle with the third strand, and push about fifteen seeds on to it.

7 Thread all three strands back through the needle and push on about fifteen melon seeds.

8 Now thread the first strand through the needle and repeat the steps as before. Continue threading the seeds in this way until the necklace is the length you want it. To finish, all three strands should be pushed through some melon seeds. Then tie the cotton strands at each end of the necklace together.

Try making necklaces from single strands of seeds that are twisted together.

If you cannot collect enough seeds for a necklace, you can make a bracelet with the seeds from one melon. Use shirring elastic instead of cotton thread.

Appliqué fruit bag

Appliqué is one of the oldest known types of embroidery, where fabric shapes are sewn onto material to make a collage. It's thought to have been invented by the ancient Chinese, who wanted to patch holes in worn-out clothes.

This appliquéd wall hanging is from Mexico.

Try making a bag decorated with appliquéd fruit shapes

You will need:
- a pencil and paper
- chalk
- a needle
- pins
- a safety pin
- scissors
- different colored felt pieces
- cotton and embroidery thread
- a length of cord approximately 3 feet (1 meter)
- a rectangle of backing cloth that won't fray, approximately 11 in. x 18 in. (28 cm x 46 cm)

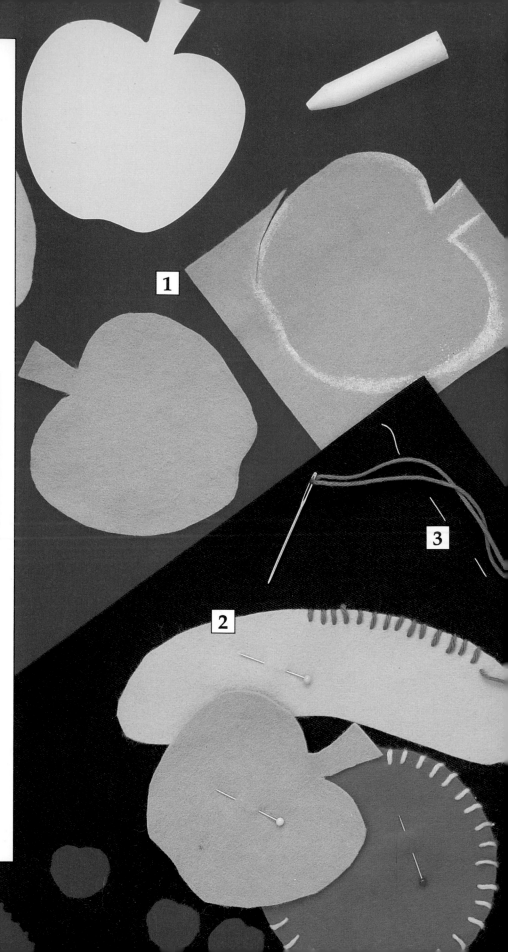

1 Fold the backing cloth in half. Think about your fruit design, which will fit on half the cloth. Sketch one or two fruits on paper first so that you get an idea of the size of the shapes you need.

Chalk fruit shapes onto the back of the felt. Cut out the shapes. Turn them over so you can't see any chalk marks.

2 Arrange the fruit shapes on the cloth so that some of the shapes overlap each other. Pin or make a loose stitch in the middle of each shape.

3 Start with a shape at the top and sew around only the edge of the shape that you can see, as shown. Then move to another shape, again sewing around only the edge that you can see. Sew all the shapes to the cloth in this way.

4 To make the picture into a bag, turn the cloth picture-side down. Fold the top of the cloth over toward you by about 1-1/2 inches (4 cm) and pin or tack in place. Stitch along the edge with small, close stitches.

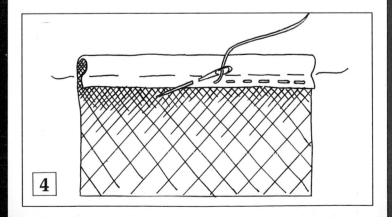

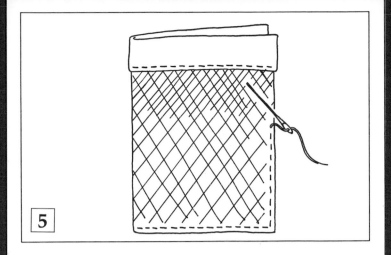

5 Fold the backing cloth in half, so that the picture is inside. Stitch the bottom edges together, then stitch the side edges together. Leave the openings in the top free.

6 Turn the bag the right way out. Fasten one end of the cord to the safety pin. Push it into one of the openings in the top hem. Push it through until it comes out the other end. Sew or tie the ends of the cord together.

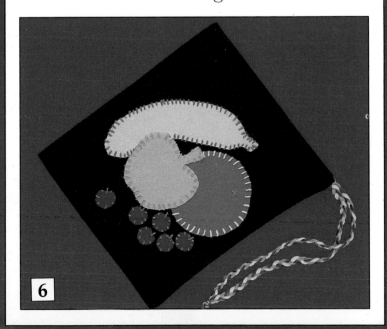

Musical instruments

Often, musical instruments are made out of fruit and seeds. In many parts of Africa, dried gourds, which are fruits, are made into shakers and maracas. In the Caribbean, coconut shells are used to make musical instruments called guiros. The outside of the coconut shell is cut with grooves, then a stick is scraped across the ridges in time to the beat of the music.

In South America, a musical instrument called a rainmaker is made from a hollow bamboo cane with sticks pushed through it. Dried corn is put in the cane, which is then sealed at both ends. Then the ends of the sticks are cut off. When the cane is turned upside down, the corn falls all the way down the tube, tumbling over the sticks, making a sound like rain.

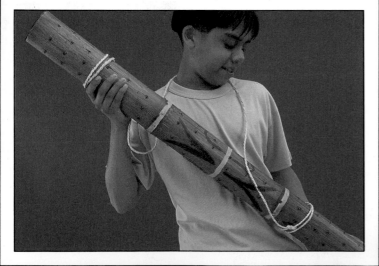

Try making your own rainmaker

You will need:
- about forty Popsicle or craft sticks
- sharp scissors
- a handful of dried chickpeas
- paintbrushes
- paints
- a cardboard tube with a lid for each end (or lids made from cardboard and transparent tape)

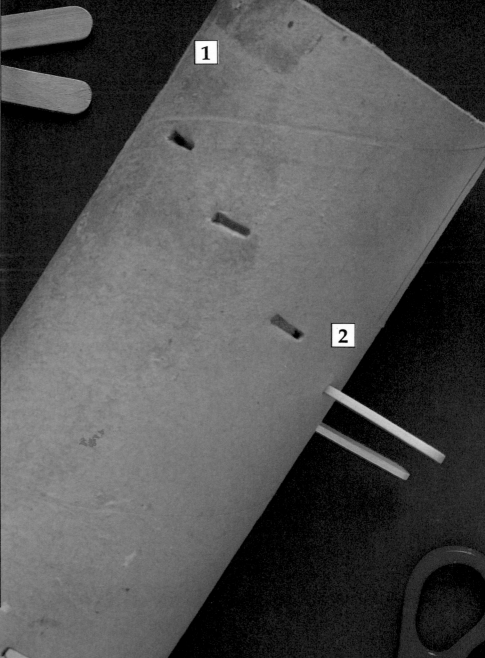

1 **Ask an adult to help you make slits in the tube.** Hold the scissors with the blades together, pointed away from your body, and make a slit in the tube. A Popsicle stick should fit tightly in the slit. Make a spiral pattern of slits in the tube.

2 Push a Popsicle stick into the first slit until it touches the other side of the tube. Put a Popsicle stick into each slit.

3 Put one lid on one end of the tube or cover with a cardboard circle and transparent tape. Place a big handful of dried chickpeas into the tube. Put the other lid on the other end of the tube or seal it with cardboard and transparent tape.

4 Paint and decorate your rainmaker.

Turn your rainmaker upside down and listen to the sound it makes. Try making a rainmaker with a different sized tube and a different amount of chickpeas. Can you make the sound of heavy rain or a light shower?

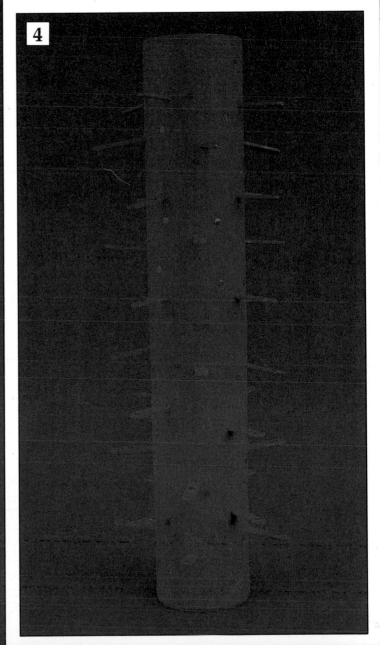

Rangoli patterns

Rangoli patterns are made from colored flour paste, rice, and spices. They are a traditional way of decorating Hindu homes for celebrations and festivals.

During the Diwali festival, rangoli patterns are made at home entrances to welcome the Goddess Lakshmi, who is said to bring health and happiness. At weddings, rangoli patterns often decorate the place where the bride and groom sit. Traditional rangoli floor designs are usually based on the lotus flower and the mango leaf.

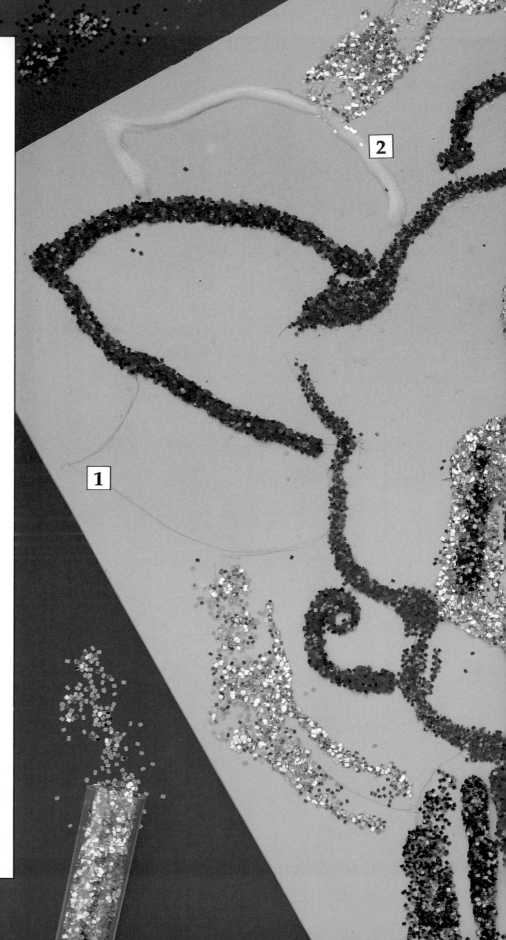

Try making a rangoli pattern with glitter

You will need:
- paper
- white glue
- a pencil
- lots of newspaper
- a paintbrush
- different colored glitters

Note: Some craft stores sell a special glitter glue. You may want to try this instead.

1 This activity can be messy, so put lots of old newspapers on your work surface before you begin. Draw your design in pencil on a piece of paper.

2 Carefully paint or squeeze a thin line of glue over part of the pencil design.

3 Hold the tube of glitter and pour it over the line of glue. Carefully tip up your glitter design on to another piece of paper and shake off any spare glitter. Make a small paper funnel and pour the spare glitter back into the tube. Continue applying different colored glitters to your pattern in this way.

3

23

A Mexican piñata

A piñata is a Mexican papier-mâché toy that is filled with sweets, fruits, nuts, and small presents. But this toy is unusual because it is meant to be broken, especially at parties and Christmastime. Sometimes piñatas are made in the shapes of animals and cartoon characters and hung from branches and posts. Everyone sings a song while one blindfolded child tries to hit the piñata with a big stick. When the piñata breaks, everyone tries to catch the treats that fall to the ground.

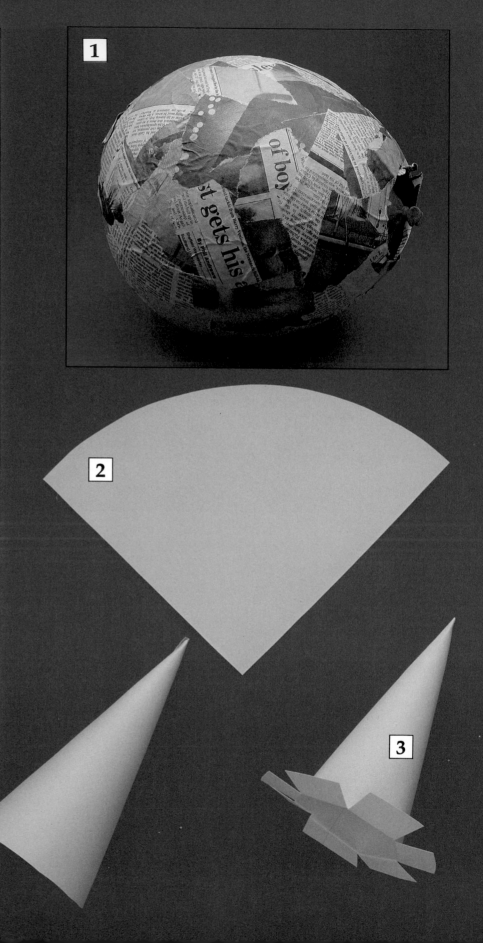

Try making a piñata for a party

You will need:
- a large balloon
- a thick brush
- a pair of compasses
- scissors
- transparent tape
- paints
- paintbrushes
- newspaper torn into strips
- sweets, nuts, and small presents
- a small bowl of wallpaper paste without fungicide

1 Blow up the balloon and tie the end. Dip a piece of newspaper into the paste and then place it on the balloon. Cover the balloon with pasted paper, overlapping the pieces slightly to make a smooth surface. At the end of the balloon, near the tie, leave a circle uncovered with a diameter of approximately 3 inches (8 cm). Cover the balloon with four layers of paper. When the papier-mâché is dry, burst the balloon.

2 Cut out a cardboard quarter-circle with a radius of about 9-1/2 inches (24 cm). Make the quarter-circle into a cone shape and glue the sides together. Make more cones in this way. One of your cones must be big enough to cover the hole in the papier-mâché balloon.

3 Make small cuts around the base of the cones and fold up the flaps.

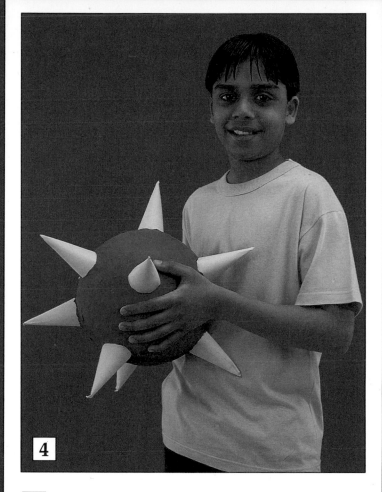

4

4 Glue and then papier-mâché the cones to the balloon. Fill the piñata with your sweets, nuts, and small presents. Then seal the hole in the end of the balloon with the last cone. Paint and decorate your piñata.

Hansel and Gretel

Food plays an important part in stories from around the world. In the story of Hansel and Gretel, two children lost in the woods suddenly come across a gingerbread house.

Try making a gingerbread house. If you get together with friends, you can make a gingerbread village. First you need to make the gingerbread shapes. Ask an adult to help you make the gingerbread. Pages 28-29 will show you how to make the gingerbread pieces into houses.

You will need:

- a pencil and paper
- scissors
- a mixing bowl
- a small bowl
- a wooden spoon
- a sieve
- a rolling pin
- a knife
- a pastry brush
- oven gloves
- a greased cookie sheet
- a wire rack
- an oven set to 400°F (200°C)

- one egg
- 1 cup (225 g) plain flour
- 1/2 cup (100 g) soft brown sugar
- 1/2 cup (100 g) margarine
- 1 teaspoon (5 ml) allspice
- 3 teaspoons (15 ml) honey
- 2 teaspoons (10 ml) ground ginger

1 To make a simple house, you will need to cut from paper two of each of the shapes shown here.

roof 1-1/2 in. (4 cm)

4 in. (10 cm)

wall 2-3/8 in. (6 cm)

4 in. (10 cm)

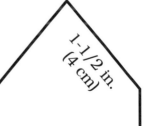

1-1/2 in. (4 cm)

side of house

2 in. (5 cm)

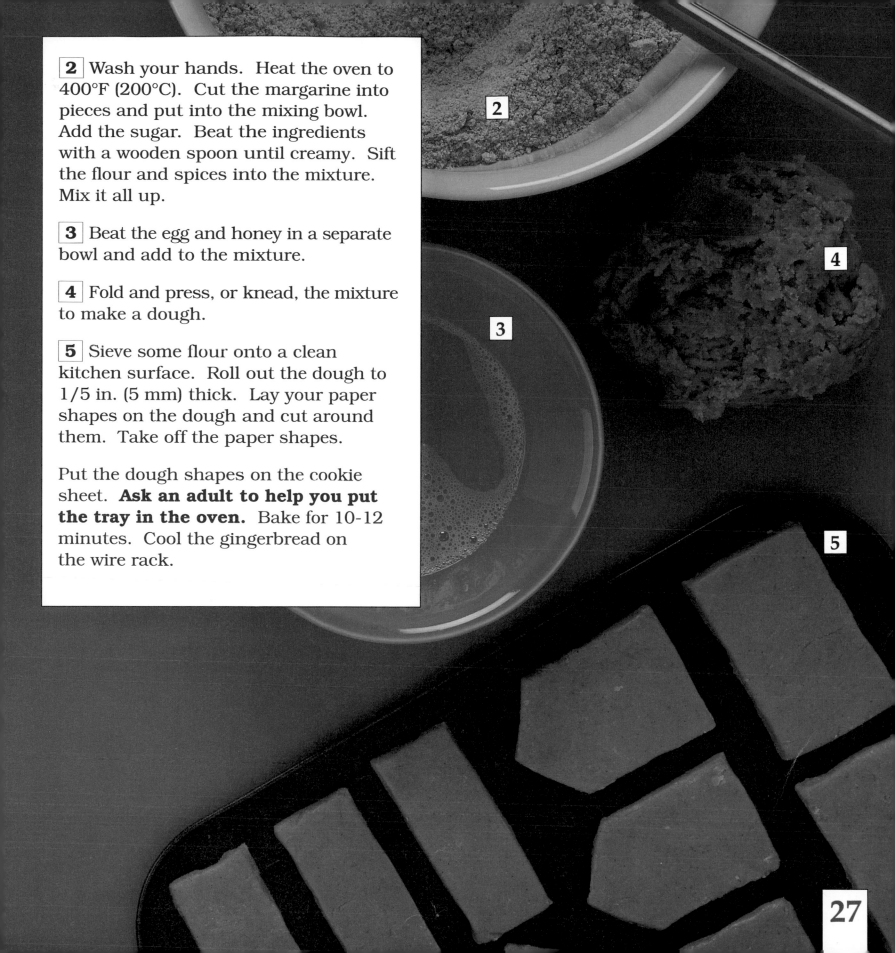

2 Wash your hands. Heat the oven to 400°F (200°C). Cut the margarine into pieces and put into the mixing bowl. Add the sugar. Beat the ingredients with a wooden spoon until creamy. Sift the flour and spices into the mixture. Mix it all up.

3 Beat the egg and honey in a separate bowl and add to the mixture.

4 Fold and press, or knead, the mixture to make a dough.

5 Sieve some flour onto a clean kitchen surface. Roll out the dough to 1/5 in. (5 mm) thick. Lay your paper shapes on the dough and cut around them. Take off the paper shapes.

Put the dough shapes on the cookie sheet. **Ask an adult to help you put the tray in the oven.** Bake for 10-12 minutes. Cool the gingerbread on the wire rack.

A gingerbread village

You will need:
- a mixing bowl
- a wooden spoon
- powdered sugar
- water
- a teaspoon
- almond paste
- a pastry brush
- dried fruit and sweets for decoration
- gingerbread pieces

1 Add a little bit of water to the powdered sugar to make a thick paste.

Brush some of the paste on the edge of the sides of one of the gingerbread pieces. Press it against the edge of one of the sides of the other pieces. Hold them together for about one minute.

2 Join the gingerbread pieces together in this way to make a house. If the house is a bit wobbly, you can use almond paste to hold the walls together.

3 There are lots of ways you can decorate your house. Use the powdered sugar paste to stick dried fruit and sweets onto the roof.

Try to make a different shaped building, but keep the shapes simple and make sure the pieces fit together.

More things to think about

This book shows you how to make and model salt dough and papier-mâché, how to print paper, and how to dye fabric. You can use these different craft techniques to make your own crafts based on food.

To get some ideas for making your own crafts, think about some of the different kinds of food in the world, how it is grown, prepared, cooked, and eaten. Think of the difference between raw and cooked food, or the number of different ways that food, such as eggs or potatoes, can be prepared. Why do you think we eat different kinds of food in the morning, afternoon, and evening?

Many cultures use food as a craft medium, but it's important to remember that food is for eating. Always ask permission before using any type of food as a craft material. Try to use food as the inspiration for your craft project, rather than making objects from it.

Visit your local art gallery, museum, or crafts center to see how artists have shown food now and in the past. In the sixteenth century, an Italian artist called Arcomboldo painted pictures that were collages of fruits, vegetables, and flowers. Try to find some of Arcomboldo's pictures in the library.

Every country has its own customs and traditions, and many are based on food. Think of all the special meals that are associated with festivals. In many religious festivals, people fast for a time and then feast on specially prepared food. Harvest festival celebrates the growing and reaping of food. It's celebrated in many different ways around the world. Do you take part in any traditions and customs at mealtimes?

Before you make your craft project, think about the best craft technique to use. For example, you could model salt dough or papier-mâché or print or dye fabric. Do you want the finished object to be flat or three-dimensional? Do you want it to have moving parts or hang from the wall? When you have answered these and similar questions, think carefully about the best way of making your project and the best materials to use.

Experiment with different kinds of decorations for your craft item. Think about the size, shape, and texture of different sorts of food. Can you create similar textures with paper, cloth, or by modeling salt dough or papier-mâché?

For more information

More books to read

Adventures in Art
    Susan Milford (Williamson)

Fun Food
    Sara Lynn and Diane James
    (Bantam)

Fun with Paint
    Moira Butterfield (Random House)

Kids Create
    Laurie Carlson (Williamson)

The Kids Multicultural Art Book
    Alexandra M. Terzian
    (Williamson)

Making Presents
    Juliet Bawden (Random House)

Making Prints
    Deri Robins (Kingfisher)

My First Cookbook
    Angela Wilkes (Knopf)

Paint
    Kim Solga (North Light)

The Paint Book
    Hannah Tofts (Simon & Schuster)

Prints
    Judy Ann Sadler (Kids Can)

Round the World Cookbook
    Caroline Young (Usborne)

60 Art Projects for Children
    Jeannette M. Baumgardner
    (Clarkson Potter)

Videos

Don't Eat the Pictures
    (Children's Television Workshop)

My First Activity Video (Sony)

My First Cooking Video (Sony)

R is for Rice (Handel Film Corporation)

What's Cooking? (Churchill Films)

Places to visit

The following places have major collections of crafts from around the world. Don't forget to look in your area museum, too.

Canadian Museum of Civilization
100 Laurier Street
P.O. Box 3100, Station B
Hull, Quebec
J8X 4H2

Denver Museum of Natural History
2001 Colorado Boulevard
Denver, Colorado 80205

Franklin Institute
20th Street and the Franklin Parkway
Philadelphia, Pennsylvania 19103-1194

Royal British Columbia Museum
675 Belleville Street
Victoria, British Columbia
V8V 1X4

The Smithsonian Institution
1000 Jefferson Drive SW
Washington, D.C. 20560

Index

For a free color catalog describing Gareth Stevens' list of high-quality books, call 1-800-542-2595 (USA) or 1-800-461-9120 (Canada). Gareth Stevens' Fax: (414) 225-0377.

Library of Congress
Cataloging-in-Publication Data
Deshpande, Chris.
    Food crafts/Chris Deshpande; photographs by Zul Mukhida.
    North American ed.
      p.   cm. — (Worldwide crafts)
    Includes bibliographical references and index.
    ISBN 0-8368-1154-2
    1. Handicraft—Juvenile literature. 2. Nature craft—Juvenile literature. 3. Food in art—Juvenile literature. [1. Handicraft. 2. Nature craft. 3. Food in art.] I. Mukhida, Zul, ill. II. Title. III. Series.
TT160.D382   1994
745.5—dc20   94-11430

North American edition first published in 1994 by
Gareth Stevens Publishing
1555 North RiverCenter Drive, Suite 201
Milwaukee, Wisconsin 53212, USA

First published in 1993 by A & C Black (Publishers) Limited, London; © 1993 A & C Black (Publishers) Limited.

Acknowledgments
Line drawings by Barbara Pegg.
Photographs by Zul Mukhida, except for: p. 12, p. 18 Life File Photographic Agency; p. 22 Format Photographic Agency; p. 24 Mexican Ministry of Tourism.

Grateful thanks to Langford and Hill, Ltd., London, for supplying all art materials.

Crafts made by Tracy Brunt except for those on pp. 14-15, 20-21, which were made by Dorothy Moir.

Printed in the United States of America

  3 4 5 6 7 8 9 9 99 98 97

At this time, Gareth Stevens, Inc., does not use 100 percent recycled paper, although the paper used in our books does contain about 30 percent recycled fiber. This decision was made after a careful study of current recycling procedures revealed their dubious environmental benefits. We will continue to explore recycling options.